LISTENING
THROUGH
THE BONE

LISTENING THROUGH THE BONE

COLLECTED POEMS

Willy Conley

Gallaudet University Press
Washington, DC

Gallaudet University Press
Washington, DC 20002
http://gupress.gallaudet.edu

Printed in the United States of America

Library of Congress Cataloging-in-Publication Data

Names: Conley, Willy, author.
Title: Listening through the bone : collected poems / Willy Conley.
Description: Washington, DC : Gallaudet University Press, 2018.
Identifiers: LCCN 2018028329 | ISBN 9781944838416 (pbk. : alk. paper) | ISBN
  9781944838423 (e-book)
Classification: LCC PS3603.O536 A6 2018 | DDC 811/.6—dc23
LC record available at https://lccn.loc.gov/2018028329

∞ This paper meets the requirements of
ANSI/NISO Z39.48-1992 (Permanence of Paper).

For Ingrid,

who knows the many treasures in an oyster

Contents

List of Photographs   xi
Acknowledgments   xiii
Introduction   1

I. INAUDIBLES

A Deaf Baptism   9
The Honeybee Epiphany   10
Salt in the Basement   11
Claustrophobic Audism of a Tenderfoot   15
The Turtle Bowl   16
The Cycle of the X-Ray Technician   18
Deaf People Don't Do Voice-overs (Hearing Envy)   19
Room Disservice   21
The Air Conditioner   22
The Deaf Simpleton   23
Debunking "Deaf Mute"   25
Will   26
ASL, Eyesdropping   28
The Miller of Moments   29
Deaf Director to a Deaf Actor   31
The Ivoryton Inn   32
The Universal Drum   35
Adam   39
Sunrise in Santa Fe with Clay   40
My Sojourn in Cathédrale Notre-Dame de Paris   42
    by Debbie Rennie, translation by Willy Conley

II. EXISTENTIALS

Verisimilitude versus Vicissitude   47
The water falls.   48

One Frame at a Time   50

I of the Beholder   51

Fibers of Time   52

Windows   54

Someone's Daughter   56

The Pop Tart & the Computer Scientist   57

Wake of the Future   59

The Relativity of Banality   60

N-u-i in South Baltimore   61

Sun, the Savior   63

The Silent Witness of Mauthausen   64

III.   QUIZZICALS

Trans-Portation   69

Volare   70

The Reverse Pavlov Effect   71

Uncarved Epitaphs   73

My Subconscious Dreams a Poem   74

The Seven-Hundred-Dollar Louis Vuitton Fountain Pen   75

Arson   76

The Missing Tipping Point   77

Origin of a Pratfall   78

Keep Politics Out of Sushi   79

Support Group   80

The Absentminded Tooth Fairy   81

How to Make Fire   83

The Proof of the Pudding   85

A Life Hack   86

IV.   IRREVOCABLES

The Perfect Woman   89

The Morning Paper   90

The Cryptology of Love   92

Alone and Breathing   93

The Way He Sees Her   95
The Eyes of Ingrid Isabella   97
November Rust   98
Missing Children   99
  by Debbie Rennie, translation by Willy Conley
Yew in the Family Plot   103
Uncle George   104

V. ENVIRONMENTALS

Five Haiku   107
A Maryland Eastern Shore Life   109
The Breezy Logic of a Nine-Year-Old   110
Family Happy Hour on Christmas Day   112
Nature Photography   113
A Long Way from a Leper Colony   115
Olfactophobia   116
Juniper, Pine, Mesquite   117
The Canyon   119
Vaudeville in the Insect World   120
Subterranea   123
The Jay   125
Impressions   126
Land of Lost Pets   127
Listening through the Bone   128

Photographs

"Peace Lily"   Frontispiece

I. INAUDIBLES

Untitled   7
"Ducks Over San Remo"   8
"Reaching for the Light of the World"   14
"Sea Turtle"   16
"Old Hearing Privilege"   20
"Hearing Aid Oasis"   27
Untitled   29
"Backstage, Engine House Theatre, Madrid, NM"   31
"Morning Along the Turquoise Trail"   40

II. EXISTENTIALS

Untitled   45
Untitled   46
"The water falls."   48
"Sun Dial, Lyme, CT"   52
"Windows Into Taos Pueblo"   55
Untitled   56
Untitled   62
"The Silent Witness"   64

III. QUIZZICALS

"Entrance to Nowhere"   67
"Steps Beach"   68
"Highway 87, Bolivar Peninsula, Texas"   70
"Unmarked Grave, Truchas, NM"   72
"Dinosaur Tracks on the Navajo Nation, Tuba City, AZ."   82
"Terrace Motel, Elkridge, MD"   86

IV. Irrevocables

"Worn Out Cowboy Boots"   87
"Segregation"   88
"The Mannequin Massacre"   91
"Old Teacup Ride, Glen Echo Park, MD"   92
"Aerial Desertscape"   97
"Family Plot, Dames Quarter, MD"   103
"After a Trot Line Run"   104

V. Environmentals

"Symbiosis"   105
"Coyote Jawbone"   106
"Lightning Indeed Strikes Twice"   108
"Empty Osprey Perch"   109
"Tangier Sound, MD"   110
"Armadillo Skull"   114
"Luna Moth"   120
"Nightdreaming on the Subway"   122
"U.S. Flag at Storm King, NY"   128
"Cow Skeleton, Abiquiu, NM"   130

Acknowledgments

I wish to thank my past and present teachers, who have instilled a sense of poetry in me, no matter how great or small: Derek Walcott, Natalie Goldberg, Juanita Rockwell, David Hays, Robert Panara, Loy Golladay, Dorothy Miles, Patrick Graybill, Sam Abrams, Stephen Policoff, James Selby, Shanny Mow, John Lee Clark, Herbert Gantschacher, Tim McCarty, Mark Jaster, Shizumi Shigeto-Manale, my parents Perry and Kitty Conley, and my son, Clayton, whom I can always rely on for an honest reaction to my poems. Tack så mycket [*thank you very much, in Swedish*] to Debbie Rennie for letting me translate a couple of her magnificent ASL poems. Special thanks to Pia Taavila, a phenomenal poet, for her eagle eye in reviewing my manuscript, and for having been a strong supporter of my poetry. And, a heapload of thanks to Ivey Wallace, director of the Gallaudet University Press and a true champion of my writings and my photography, for her deft hand in editing this book and bringing it to fruition. Much gratitude goes to Alexa Selph for spiffing up my manuscript while furthering my education in poetry, and to Deirdre Mullervy, managing editor at Gallaudet University Press, for seeing the book through the final stages of production.

PUBLICATIONS

I would like to express my gratitude to the editors of the following publications in which these poems and photos first appeared, in some cases in a slightly different form:

Poems

- *The Deaf Heart*: "Cracking the Cryptology of Love" and "Trans-Portation," Gallaudet University Press.

- *Deaf Lit Extravaganza*: "The Ivoryton Inn," Handtype Press.

- *Deaf American Poetry*: "A Deaf Baptism," "Salt in the Basement," and "The Miller of Moments," Gallaudet University Press.

- *No Walls of Stone—An Anthology of Literature by Deaf and Hard of Hearing Writers*: "One Frame Per Second," Gallaudet University Press.

- *The Deaf Way II Anthology*: "The Perfect Woman," "Cycle of the X-Ray Technician," and "Salt in the Basement," Gallaudet University Press.

- *The Tactile Mind Press: Kindred*: "The water falls.," The Tactile Mind Press.

- *Vignettes of the Deaf Character and Other Plays*: "Salt in the Basement," "The Universal Drum," and "The water falls.," Gallaudet University Press.

- *The Washington Post*: "The Honeybee Epiphany" (originally titled "Autobiography as Haiku").

- *Modern Haiku*: "Coyote Bones" (see "Five Haiku").

- *Theatre for Young Audiences Today*: "The Universal Drum." Imagination Stage commissioned the writing of this dramatic poem as a performance piece for the Deaf Access Company in 2002.

- *Organs of Vision and Speech*: "A Maryland Eastern Shore Life."

- *ICON*: "I of the Beholder," "November Rust," and "Someone's Daughter."

Photographs

- *Big Muddy* (2013): "Segregation," "Sundial."

- *Sheepshead Review* (Fall 2012): "The Mannequin Murders."

- *Carolina Quarterly* (Fall 2012): "Old Hearing Privilege" (formerly "Dinosaurs").

- *20x20 Magazine* (2012): "Terrace Motel."

- *34th Parallel* (2009): "Night Dreaming."

- *The Tactile Mind: Kindred* (Autumn 2002): "The water falls.," The Tactile Mind Press.

- *Deaf Studies Digital Journal* (Spring 2014): "Deaf Adult Gone" (now untitled); "Old Hearing Privilege"; "Who's Listening" (now "Hearing Aid Oasis"); and "Backstage, Engine House Theatre, Madrid, NM."

Introduction

Having been profoundly deaf since birth (105-decibel loss in the left ear and 98 decibels in the other), I don't write "with the ear" as most poets do, but with the eye. As Deaf people are apt to do, I have become attuned to our world through tactile means, listening through the bone for vibrations, sensing shifts in air currents, recognizing wafting odors, and observing fluctuations and reflections of light and movements in the water.

I've worn hearing aids since I was three, which was when my parents discovered I was deaf. It may seem ironic, but I have always loved the various sounds of life: voices, music, nature, and vehicles. I was always asking people to help me identify unfamiliar sounds. An audiologist once noted that my residual hearing—what little I have of it—revealed clear discrimination, meaning that there was hardly any distortion in the way I heard things whenever I had my hearing aids on.

I often love silence and would go for days without wearing my hearing aids. But, when that happens, it is not really total silence because tinnitus—my inner radio—comes on. It is a twenty-four-hour, self-powered radio without control knobs that cannot be unplugged. Sometimes the sounds are musical and soothing while at other times they're downright annoying.

How does this relate to the way I write poems? I see the world through Deaf eyes. Yet, I also hear the world filtered through my faulty ear-drum-hammer-anvil-stirrup-cochlea mechanism, sometimes greatly amplified by a Phonak Naidu Q-50 digital device hanging behind my ear like a flesh-colored slug.

The crux of a lot of my poems comes to me rather quickly. When I look at an object—a hawk, a shoe, or a bone—it forms a latent poem rapidly in my head. If I don't write it down somewhere soon, it's gone. A good number of latent poems have appeared in dreams. From the late-night, half-awake scribbles, it becomes a matter of adding on to the core images and letting the hands of my brain shape them in whatever form they desire.

Influenced by my background in photography, I tend to write poems that are imagistic, clear, and precise, often with mood lighting. If they could be painted, I would say they were Hopper-esque.

My earliest exposure to poetry was probably as a kid reading nursery rhymes. In "Jack and Jill," I remember being disturbed by the image of Jack cracking open his head and exposing his brain when he fell down the hill. Then in the 1970s as a teen, I would read poetry in *MAD* magazines, which often published goofy, satirical poems. I recall this one by heart:

> Roses are red,
> violets are blue.
> We make our bread
> on clods like you.

I remember taking my first creative writing course in college. My teacher wrote this short poem on the board one day, which I've never forgotten:

> Hooray, hooray for the first of May,
> outdoor fucking begins today.

I had a notetaker for this course who wrote this out in her notes with metrical markings above the words to illustrate the rhythm of this short poem. What a way to learn about couplets!

Whenever I was away from home, I wrote sappy tribute poems to my mother and father on Mother's Day and Father's Day. One of my Mother's Day poems was submitted to what I thought was a decent poetry writing competition only to learn that I had to pay for my own poem to be published. Eventually a copy of the book was sent to me with my poem in it. Of course, it was one of those fly-by-night publishers who basically photocopied or retyped all of the poems and stapled them together inside some colored card stock with a title slapped on it. Nevertheless, I was proud to see my poem and name in print within a book, even if it was a collection of photocopies.

I believe a part of my learning about poems happened on a subconscious level from memorizing lyrics to songs that I loved growing up. My cousins got me turned on to Alice Cooper. He happened to be one of the few musicians during the seventies who included lyrics on some of his LP record sleeves. A favorite song of mine, "I'm Eighteen," still sticks with me to this day:

> I got a baby's brain and an old man's heart,
> took eighteen years to get this far.

And then there was another favorite, "American Pie" by Don McLean:

> Bye, bye Miss American Pie.
> Drove my Chevy to the levee but the levee was dry.

I was constantly memorizing lyrics, trying to follow the vocals on songs playing from my parents' record player. Since I had grown up not knowing any other Deaf people (other than my younger sister), I was fully immersed in a hearing world. My friends were hearing, my parents were hearing, and the public schools that I went to had all hearing students and teachers. As has always been true, listening to music and singing along with it were popular among my hearing friends and school peers. Knowing that I couldn't carry a tune in a bucket, the closest I could come to singing along was to lip-sync. As long as I was accurately lip-syncing and following a song's rhythm, I was able to get by in hearing circles. This, I believe, was how poetry began to become ingrained in my head.

I attempted to write some of my own songs, but they never got further than a verse here or there. This is one I wrote from my summer days as a teenager hanging out in Ocean City, Maryland:

> Saw some gorgeous ladies
> in a blue Mercedes;
> they was headin' for
> the Back of the Rack.

Taking literature courses in college introduced me to reading poems on a deeper level. And getting involved in theater as an actor introduced me to even more poems, since our performing material often dealt with poetic language.

The death of my grandmother, and the suicide of my grandfather six months later, hit me hard. Feeling a strong need to write about them, I found poetry to be a comfortable vehicle to transport my feelings about their passing as noted in "The water falls." and "One Frame at a Time." After graduating from college, I went on to write short fiction and plays, but I found poetry to be a close friend who was always there for brief correspondences or late-night chats.

During the early years of my work as a professional actor with the National Technical Institute for the Deaf's Sunshine Too, the Fairmount Theatre of the Deaf, and later with the National Theatre of the Deaf, we were sometimes expected to perform poems in ASL. With Sunshine Too, I performed the wonderfully insightful poem "On His Deafness," by my former professor Robert Panara, as part of the variety show we presented on national tour. Not only was I blown away by the poem's simplicity and imagery, I was also struck by how a Deaf poet had such awareness of sound: "the tinkle of a bell, the cooing of a dove, the swish of leaves, the raindrop's pitter-patter on the eaves." And I'll never forget the delightful paradox of the poem's final line, "And if I choose, the rustle of a star!"

Later I learned that Panara had lost his hearing at the age of ten from spinal meningitis. As a result of that, he began experiencing head noises, which was actually tinnitus. He loved to listen to his "secret radio." Sometimes while lipreading someone, he imagined the voice that person had, or while reading a book, he heard a voice speaking the words. As he became older, he read poetry from some of the greats—Blake, Keats, Kipling, Pope, Shakespeare. As he read their writings, he listened to how their imagined voices reverberated in his mind. This influenced the way he wrote some of his poems, which originated in the melodies and sounds from the secret radio in his head.

The National Theatre of the Deaf occasionally performed children's shows, which were varietal in nature. One of the poems I had to act out and perform in ASL was e. e. cummings's hauntingly sweet poem about a "little lame balloonman who whistles far and wee." Cummings's poetry writing style showed me that poems didn't always have to rhyme, have proper capitalization and punctuation, or be spaced and structured in any formal way on the page. "Language for the Eye," one of Dorothy Miles's most famous poems, was another one that I occasionally performed. This Deaf poet created an ingenious blend of English and signs that lent itself well to sign play as evidenced in one of the lines in the poem: "Hold a tree in the palm of your hand, Or topple it with a crash."

While on theater tours, I often spent my free time exploring the towns we stayed in, and their bookstores, and then, later, writing in my motel room. I felt a particular kinship with the writer Sam Shepard, an actor, playwright, and director who also wrote fiction and poetry. I was always seeking out his writings on bookshelves. I came across his collection of poems, essays, and short fiction in the books *Hawk Moon* and *Motel Chronicles*.

His poems were often imagistic, dark, stark, ironic, realistic, unsentimental, and, at times, slyly humorous. Raymond Carver's poems were similar in nature, and I came to appreciate his work as well. Then I happened across the writings of Richard Brautigan, whose fiction and poems were deceptively simple, unpretentious, sometimes absurd, and accessible. These three writers were strong influences on the way I write my poems.

On writing the poems involving the Deaf experience (in the section "Inaudibles"), I found that the creative process added an extra layer of joy. Making the Deaf connection was like discovering an Easter egg or more cool stuff in my Christmas stocking. Even though I learned ASL in college, I was able to imagine a childhood reverie in ASL and capture its likeness on paper in English; "Salt in the Basement" allowed me to explore that. I felt a pleasurable power in being able to create sound effects on the page and clear up a world-renowned misconception in "Debunking 'Deaf Mute,'" or poke the eye of the hearing world at the lack of universal access to hotel amenities in "Room Disservice." And I thoroughly enjoyed translating into English Debbie Rennie's ASL poem about a visit to the Notre-Dame Cathedral in Paris and having a conversation with Quasimodo, the deaf, hunchbacked bellringer.

I still keep in mind Panara's advice to aspiring Deaf poets: "Never fear the use of 'free verse' when you cannot hear," and "Take care your sentiments are not too fruity." Yet throughout all of this, I'm not so much expressing what I see, or hear, with what little hearing I have, but more what I am feeling in my bones.

I. Inaudibles

A Deaf Baptism

A family of mallards
by a waterfall's green ledge
paddling
preening
shivering off waterbugs.
A feather or two comes loose
and floats over the water's edge.

Suddenly a duckling
chasing after a feather
flapping
jerking
toppling over the waterfall.
Lost, it struggles through
the curtain into the world of white water.

The Honeybee Epiphany

An autumn afternoon in first grade.
I felt a tickle behind my ear,
brushed it away. I must have yelped
because my teacher rushed over
and pointed to a honeybee on the floor.
I didn't understand. She gestured
for me to take out my "things."
I pulled out my hearing aids,
which emitted high-pitched feedback.
Everyone stared while she coated my ear
with baking soda. I looked at the dying bee,
not realizing that moment
would be the beginning
of many years of jeers
about my deafness.

Salt in the Basement

—An American Sign Language reverie in English

happen summer
me little, almost high wash-wash machine
down basement, me have blue car
drive drive round round
basement

me drive every corner
drive drive drive
then BOOM! me crash

there tall paper brown round
me get out car
look inside brown round tall
many many small small
white rock rock
small white rock rock

for-for?

me put white rock rock
in mouth
very very salty
same-same Grandma
mashed-mashed potato

me back inside blue car
drive drive round round
basement

happen winter
father down basement
go to brown round tall
father shovel big lump
there white rock rock
many white rock rock

father told me for-for
outside road

me ask again for-for?
me outside blue car, cold cold
drive drive straight straight
me watch father

white rock rock father throw throw
on walk-walk
father his brown car
throw white rock rock
throw round throw round

me ask father for-for?

father say for mother
white rock rock for mother?

me get out blue car
me look down white rock rock
burn burn hole many many
hole in ice
same-same ice in my lemonade

me jaw-drop
white rock rock rock
make hole in ice break-break
same-same make hole in my tummy?

that why me pee-pee
poo-poo always?

me no more eat
white rock rock
inside basement

me remember
mother year last
happen winter
mother outside
ice all-over
mother fall
arm broke
father told me
go down basement
stay stay
me inside blue car
drive round round
basement

Claustrophobic Audism of a Tenderfoot

Away at a mountaintop winter camp,
six Boy Scouts bunked in a cabin.

At lights-out, I lay awake,
numb and shivering,

stifled in my sleeping bag,
severed from conversation.

My hearing aids conveyed
other guys chattering into the night,
too dark to lipread.

They laughed often,
banging against bunk beds and boards.

I stared out the window at a storage barn,
its warm light shining over
red double doors.

Fixating on the narrow pool of yellow,
buffering blackness and blather,
soothed me.

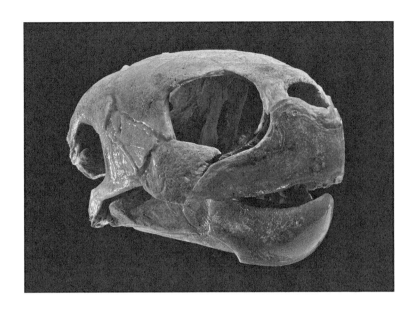

The Turtle Bowl

When he was a boy
he had, in a glass bowl,
a tiny timid turtle that often retracted
its head into a fold of skin,
like his penis when he was cold or scared.

He wore turtlenecks in elementary school;
his mother liked them on him.
During class, moments of choking sensations
made him stretch the fabric out
to his chin and hang it there
like Mort, the Bazooka Joe character.

His mother would wash the shirts
in hot water and dry them at the highest possible setting
to shrink the 'necks back to their original size.

Mr. Light, his junior high teacher, wrote in
his yearbook: "Emulate the turtle—
to go places, you must stick out your neck."

Sometimes at social gatherings
his stomach got upset.
He couldn't eat, excusing
himself to go to the bathroom or
outside for fresh air.

In his fifties he suffered pounding heart palpitations
from coffee, walking up hills, alcohol,
stress, and divorce matters.

He suspects the seeds of anxiety
began with turtlenecks—
the boa constrictor of shirts—
and being the only deaf kid
in the bowl of public school.

The Cycle of the X-Ray Technician

Whenever I feel down about my deafness,
my receding hairline, my weight,
my glaucoma, and on and on, I remind myself—
the X-ray Technician.

I passed him every time I delivered
some files to Medical Records.
He'd hang up recently processed X-rays
on the light boxes with the blue light
illuminating a badly burned and disfigured face—
the X-ray Technician.

He had one normal arm,
the other a prosthesis with a metal claw.
I'd start to feel sorry for him . . .
then I stopped myself.
I wouldn't want him to pity me—
the X-ray Technician.

For all I know, he may have his own home
with a beautiful wife, lover, or family.
He may be an excellent artist
or a freelance auto mechanic.
He may be the best bowler in Texas
or have the highest RBI on his softball team
or, he may be lonely,
feeling sorry for himself like me—
the X-ray Technician.

Deaf People Don't Do Voice-overs
(Hearing Envy)

He can't hear the voicing on TV
behind the cartoon characters
(captions aren't provided).

He tries to lipread Bugs Bunny
(classic rabbit overbite
talking while munching on a carrot),
like reading Cantonese or Braille
if you're not Chinese or blind.

He knows, in a dark studio somewhere,
a group of Hollywood actors
in Hawaiian shirts and shorts,
make a ton of money watching animation
while filling in empty cartoon bubbles
with their million-dollar voices.

Room Disservice

Next to the commode in my hotel room
is a wall phone near the toilet paper,
another phone on the desk by the stationery,
and a third phone on the nightstand.

- ✓ Answer an incoming call
- ✓ Call for more towels
- ✓ Dial up for some ice
- ✓ Punch in a wake-up call
- ✓ Ring for breakfast in bed
- ✓ Buzz for a cab
- ✓ Phone a complaint
- ✓ Alert about a burnt-out bulb
- ✓ Hit 911 for emergencies

Damn, hearing people are spoiled!

The Air Conditioner

A deaf boy who went to a deaf day school
woke up one hot spring morning to find
her across the hall, still in bed. She was supposed
to wake him up earlier to drop him off
at school. He shook her awake to no avail.

"Finish-finish, please wake up!
Finish! Wake up!" he signed.

He shook her arms, felt them cold.
He turned the knobs on the A/C unit
but it kept spewing conditioned air.
Pounding on the machine, he screamed and signed:

"Finish, finish, please—off!
She's cold! Off—now!!"

He kicked the vent, cracking a plastic rib.
Refrigerated air blew at his face. He pulled
blankets out of the closet
piling them atop the still figure.
Beside the bed he sat,
waiting for her to warm up.

Hours passed, darkness arrived.
He shuddered now and then,
rubbing his hand over the
only parent he had ever had.

The Deaf Simpleton

Masked hygienist
fastens bib
lowers him
takes X-rays
scrapes teeth
under gums
polishes teeth
flosses teeth
copper taste
blood pools
spits out
filthy bowl

masked dentist
no expression
metal pick
taps teeth
stretches mouth
tongue out
dentist and hygienist
silently confer
no cavities
thumbs up
raises me
removes bib
waves goodbye

next room
another patient
raised upright

hygienist and dentist
no masks
chatting laughing
no bib
clean bowl

Debunking "Deaf Mute"

[grunt]
[groan]
[gargle]
[gasp]
[giggle]
[chuckle]
[guffaw]
[hiss]
[sigh]
[snarl]
[snore]
[sniff]
[snort]
[sneeze]
[sob]
[pant]
[ahem]
[yawn]
[yell]
[hiccup]
[growl]
[moan]
[cheer]
[burp]
[blow]
[click]
[hum]

Will

A 105-decibel loss will get you one of these.

The culturally *Deaf* will label you "hard-of-hearing."

The politically correct will call you "hearing-impaired" or
  "non-hearing."

Some will think you can hear normally. Others will shout into
  your ears.

Feedback will go off when you hug someone.

Little kids will stare. Adults will take sidelong glances.

"Friends" will joke about alien communication.

You will get disability rates on bus and train fares, and at the
  theater.

Flight attendants will seat you away from emergency windows.

Sores will develop, and sometimes fester, on your ear.

You will sometimes get headaches and be easily distracted.

After you take them off at night, you will get tinnitus.

Your earmolds will turn brown and smelly.

Auditory signals will sound mechanical.

Sometimes you will inadvertently wash them with the laundry.

Eventually you will hear static, then get short-circuited, and then nothing.

You will fork out over $4,000 again for a new pair.

You will spend roughly $100,000 in your lifetime for these.

You will appreciate the drone of a small airplane, the roar of a train, the cars whizzing by on the freeway, the radio deejay's voice, the telephone ringing, the television blaring, people talking, ocean waves breaking, the sounds of lovemaking, and music, like Bruce Springsteen's angst-filled voice on "Nebraska"—even if you can't make out the words.

You will never be *Hearing*, though. Don't ever let anyone tell you that.

ASL, Eyesdropping

books, kiss-fist
add course? stand-on-fence
advanced calculus, mind limit
my son, I-L-Y
homework, finish-finish?
pepperoni, nose-throw
movie *Get Out*, champ
spring break, pah!
Jamaica, finish-touch
drive 90 mph, expert you
beer spilled, wrong happen
yesterday, true-biz!
her talk, vee-vee . . .
Sim-Com, hearing-mind
mini-skirt, jaw-drop
nail polish, 258
sleeping with him, me say-nothing
pregnant, funny zero
involved? hands-off
my turn, mind-disappear
grass roots march, train go sorry
no raise, swallow pride
borrow money, brown-nose
Trump, sick you!
story end—that!

The Miller of Moments

On Pattaconk Brook
in Chester, Connecticut,
up in a little tower
above the old grist mill

someone
steams rain
sifts thunder
sews lightning

squeezes sunlight
saves sign language

a pair of hands
open the wood slats

the flowers hold their scents
the brook ceases babbling
the ivy stops crawling
the wind looks back

eyes for darkness
watch below
the daily struts and frets
of drama school deaf actors
their private moments

when the sun
bows to the horizon
the hands withdraw

come morning the summer school cook
rips yesterday off the calendar
before people walk in and out
for three squares a day

no one notices
the yearly scores
of faint footprints
up on the mill tower deck

yet another day
the spirit of deaf theater
survives

Deaf Director to a Deaf Actor

—Translated from American Sign Language

> Don't worry about
> taking in everything
> at once.
>
> Let your fingers
> get the feel
> of the material.
>
> Later, we'll file
> and add polish.

The Ivoryton Inn

—in memory of Dorothy Miles

Empty bar at the Ivoryton Inn
just the bartender, me, and the TV.
The odor of stale cigarette smoke
and beer clings to everything made of wood.
This is the town where they used to ship elephant tusks
up the river and forge them into piano keys.

He's skinny with sunken cheeks, deep-set eyes.
All he wears is black. He tries to strike
a conversation but I hear nothing; I only
see mumbling lips and CNN
on the tube in the background.

I just nod.

Though no one has come in,
he constantly wipes the bar.
I order a glass of wine, and when it comes,
I make sure the glass stays
on the coaster.

I lived upstairs in this place
two summers past to interview deaf theater students
from the world over. They came to this bar
to eat, drink, and rehearse play scenes
for the drama school held in an
old renovated grist mill nearby.

Their silhouettes sit beside me, and
some with drinks in their hands
lean on the baby grand piano:

Shan from Hong Kong complains
about the lack of opportunity
for deaf actors in his country.
Anu from India isn't here to learn
about acting but ways to meet American men
and get a green card.

Loretta, the redhead, from Australia—
unaware that she has no stage presence—
thinks her flashy personality will attract all
sorts of Hollywood offers.

Tom from England studies a Pinter monologue
and drinks milk; he tries out words in
two-handed British fingerspelling.

As if it were just yesterday,
I see their facial expressions and
native sign languages,
each with its own signature and syntax.

In the early seventies
a deaf theater company won a Tony Award.
A sudden growing interest
in hiring deaf actors came about.
Hundreds and hundreds of eager deaf students
enrolled in the summer program
each one manufactured—
some against their will—

to the specs of well-known acting teachers
and directors from New York City who could hear.

I finish my wine and leave a tip
at the bar's edge. The bartender
gives me a shifty glance and then
swoops in like a vulture to grab his
money and put the wine glass away.
He wipes the entire bar again, even
though only a small area was smudged.

On the way out I touch the baby grand.
My hand trails along the curves,
stopping at the keyboard.

I strike a black key, an unknown note,
thinking about fabricated deaf actors.
I tap a white key and wonder about
the elephants in Africa or India
or wherever they were caught.

What were these humble creatures
feeling when the poachers held them down
to saw off their noble tusks?

The Universal Drum

—A dramatic, visual poem with drum accompaniment

Stage direction: An actor comes on stage rolling a short barrel, tube, and/or a large bowl. A few more people come with a flexible drum head and use it like a mini-trampoline, flinging up some object that's easy to bounce. Another person can bring on the fasteners or whatever is needed to secure the drum head over the barrel. Some could come in with bongos and tambourines. Others could use their own bodies as drumming instruments (slapping the thighs or chests, clapping hands, stomping the feet, or popping the hand against the open mouth). All of this could be done in a fun, entertaining way. One by one, the ensemble develops an entrancing beat, which leads to a funky dance.

As the dance dies down, members of the ensemble narrate this poem in American Sign Language while others voice in English, perhaps all choreographed to a drumbeat in the background. Specific percussive beats can be used to emphasize or punctuate parts of the poem.

Drum.
(*fingerspell*)
D-R-U-M.

Musical instrument
of two membranes,
called "heads"
stretched over a frame

lacing binds tightly
over the frame.

Drums
found all over the world
since 6000 B.C.
in almost every culture
the most precious of
all musical instruments.

In Africa and Europe,
certain drums symbolize royalty.

In Asia, Russia, and
Native American tribes,
drums are used for ceremonial dances.
In Deaf culture, a drum
is the one musical instrument
that reaches the heart
of a deaf person.

Drums are universal,
creating strength and solidarity,
reflecting the rhythms of life:
the dawning of a new day
the setting of night.

Trees swaying in the breeze.
The rumble of thunderstorms.
A door slamming.
People walking.
Hearts beating.
The rhythms of life.

Strike the instrument
with the hands
and we can create

(*Ensemble acts out each of the following creations*)

Music
  Rhythms
    Signals
      Marches
        Dances
          Conversations.

A drum can express
who you are
and who we are.

I'm deaf and I live
in a Deaf world.

I'm hearing and I live
in a hearing world.

(*Deaf and hearing actors, simultaneously*)

I'm Deaf and I live   I'm hearing and I live
in both worlds.   in both worlds.

     Like the drum
      we are
     woven together
     in one place—

Like the two drum heads fastened
to the frame,

tight,
our hands reach out
to both deaf and hearing worlds.

Using our drum to communicate,
we send our message to you.

(*Deaf and hearing actors, simultaneously*)

Look   Listen

        the rhythm of our family

Deaf   hearing

        equal
       connected
      united.

Adam

of the sky blue eyes
and the first name of man
my very first nephew

calls me Unca Ninny
signing a horn on the head
and "B" over the nose

he runs fast along walls
head turned inwards
to feel his life speed

Sunrise in Santa Fe with Clay

My ten-month-old son
rises at 5:30 in the morning.
I lift him out of his crib and
change his diapers.

We walk along the breezeway
of my friend's adobe
and stop in front of the large-paned windows.

One by one I raise the wood shutters.

He is awestruck by what's out there.
As each blind goes up, he leans forward
to give the window a good slap,
letting the world know he's up.

Each window around the house
has a faint little handprint as
we return to the first window.

The sun peekaboos over the horizon.
My son squints, smiles,
signing his very first word in life:

Light!
Light!
Light!

My Sojourn in Cathédrale Notre-Dame de Paris

by Debbie Rennie

—Translation from American Sign Language by Willy Conley

My eyes take in
the lofty, medieval cathedral.
They scan the statues of saints
and stop at the stunning
Saint Denis holding his decapitated head.

Visitors line the long corridor
waiting to pay the entry fee.
I pull out some coins, uncertain
of the correct amount.

A tall blond man
with a toothy grin
says something.
I give a dismissive smile
and proceed up the tower staircase.

Step by step,
winding round and round,
spiraling higher and higher,
my hand trails the walls
of Catholic stone blocks.
I see each one cut and placed there
centuries ago
by whipped, screaming slaves.

Up the narrow stairs
step by step,
winding round and round,
spiraling higher and higher
to the top of the tower,
I pass through a corridor
and a portal where gargoyles
menace oncomers.

Then, the great Bourdon Emmanuel
bell begins to peal.
I conjure up Quasimodo,
the deaf, hunchbacked bell ringer
cowering, hiding his face.

I sign to him:
"You're beautiful.
There's nothing wrong with you."

He says:
"I'm ugly—my face is deformed,
my back has a hump. Don't compare,
you are beautiful, not me."

"I'm telling you, you're beautiful inside."
Quasimodo winces, looks back,
unsure of my reality.

Emmanuel swings back and forth,
ringing over the City of Lights,
the Eiffel Tower,
and the Seine,
while a light mist falls.

The blond man bursts my reverie
with a flirty smile
about Paris' beauty. I nod,
acknowledging the obvious.

Through the portal and the long hall
I backtrack down the staircase
step by step,
winding round and round,
spiraling lower and lower.

On the ground, I absorb it all.

The man taps my shoulder,
prattling on and on.

I gesture:
"Wait—I'm deaf."
Horrified, shocked, speechless,
he scurries away.

I aim at his back
with my imaginary rifle
and blast him.

II. Existentials

Verisimilitude versus Vicissitude

When I go out in public,
occasionally I see a man
who I think
used to look like me,
              looks like me,
                        or who I will look like.

I do not like the man who I will look like.
Shocking to see him
                              not far into the future
                                        bent, fat, and gray.

The water falls.

I sit and watch the waterfall
While far from home in Selden Bay
And wonder what's going through
My grandfather's mind today.

Lying beside him,
His loving wife of fifty-five years
Fades before his eyes,
Which well and sting with tears.

Cancer cells multiply and build.
An evil metastasis marches,

Destroys everything under the skin
He so delicately touches.

She will improve, he thinks,
As he force-feeds her applesauce
Tainted with medicine—it may
As well be a spoon of moss.

He's like a child with an old, broken doll,
Trying to fix the legs and arms,
Pushing the stuffing back in,
Not realizing the material has worn.

There is hope.
It's in the hereafter
Just as water runs over the fall.

One Frame at a Time

he died

It's hard to watch my mother go
through clips of her life: grey
Polaroids of childhood, tattered
prints of her parents, her father's
army medals, her mother's jewelry

alone on a winter night

She touches each relic and stares,
a memory slides in superimposed.
She grows still and watches each
part of her past.

in his bedroom —

The object is laid back on the
table and another is held. One
memory segues to the next; her
ritual of grief. One day it will be
me touching her belongings.

shot himself, my grandfather

I of the Beholder

I lie "unconscious,"
eyes closed,
downstage, facing upstage,
my back two feet from the audience.

I have to be still.
My heart jackhammers,
my breath rattles.

The eye closest to the floor
opens a crack.
The gates in the play open.
All the characters spill out,
one by one.

I fell wrong this time.
All my weight rests
on my left arm, making my
fingers curl involuntarily.
My shin throbs.

I wiggle my toes to make sure
no bones are broken.
They're jammed inside a steel bucket
I stepped into
on purpose.

I blink away the sweat that trickles
into my eyes.

Can the audience see any of this?

Fibers of Time

I wash a week's worth of dirty laundry,
the clothes seven days older than last week.
Sudsy water swishes around
behind the glass of the front loader.

Outside the kitchen window,
the morning sun pokes
between the oak leaves.
The tree hasn't changed much.

I take out of the dryer my dungarees,
T-shirts, underwear, and socks,
their color faded from when I bought them.

I wet my fingertips and scrape
a blue-gray wad of lint out of the filter.

Every time I wash my clothes,
they're losing fiber. One day, my pants
will be nothing but a button and a zipper.
I fold my clothes, starting with the underwear first,
the socks, the T-shirts, and, last, the pants:
the same order I use to get dressed.

A squirrel scampers up the oak trunk.
I look at the palms of my hands.
They look the same, but a week ago
they were different, like my clothes.
I throw away the wad of lint.

I've got to make better use of my time.

Windows

Lying in bed
he turns over,
looks out his bedroom window:
tinges of blue and orange on the horizon
runway beacons flashing
the slow trajectory of a jetliner
rising from a nearby airport.

416 people sit,

drinking coffee
reading books & magazines
taking a shit
listening to music
crying on each other's shoulders
writing a speech
throwing up in a bag
taking a nap
playing a computer game
knitting a scarf
manning the controls
unwrapping breakfast trays
sneezing into a handkerchief
saying a prayer
snapping a photograph
filing a fingernail

while flying at 567 miles per hour
over his house this very moment.
He yawns and rolls over
to look out another window.

Someone's Daughter

a little girl's shoe
lies on the shoulder
of a Kansas highway
once pink now beaten and brown
　　　　where is she

a truck zooms by

the plastic shoe strap
flaps in the wind

Pop Tart & the Computer Scientist

—For Michael John Muss

Ever since fourth grade
I've had the jones for
a brown sugar & cinnamon Pop Tart
—unfrosted and untoasted.

One day in the cafeteria
a bespectacled student from my class—
top of the shirt buttoned
an array of pens & pencils in the pocket—
sat next to me, opened
his gray metal lunch box,
and laid out two Pop Tarts
on a napkin.

Never had I seen a sandwich
so flat and rectangular.
He offered one to me.
I took a bite, the first
of a million bites,
savoring sweet cinnamon and dough.

One day
over a morning coffee and newspaper
while biting into my Pop Tart,
I saw his picture
in an obituary,
dead from a car accident,
leaving a wife and four kids.

Worked most of his
adult life as a computer scientist
for the Army.

Wished I could've added
to his obituary:

Helped Kellogg improve the
performance of its stocks
by introducing a legendary product
to a lifelong customer.

Wake of the Future

She died the other day.

At the funeral parlor,
lying in state on a bed,
her dead eyes open,
rolling around,
lips puckered.

People milled about.

Her younger brother rose up
from the bed, to shift positions
of embrace.
Her shoulder jerked a little.
Then her older sister
came out from under the covers and put her
arms around both siblings in a group hug.

People nearby whispered to one another,
nodding heads in sympathy.

When the family was ready, they got out of
bed and straightened their clothes,
surrounded the body. The undertaker
pressed a button on the headboard.
Her eyes closed. Muscle spasms ceased.

Then they went about the business of burying her.

The Relativity of Banality

Some days he felt like an Apollo astronaut
who had touched the moon. Coming down to earth
to everyday life was unbearably,
unforgivably mundane.

It didn't take a rocket and travel to the stars
to experience that—just a bus
and a starring role on a national theater tour.

N-u-i in South Baltimore

At night, he and his cousin
roam the inner-city streets and alleys
under sickly yellow mercury vapor lights.
Drug-addicted brothers and friends
hang around Formstone row homes
with white marble steps,
waiting for a fix or a fight.
Sallow, stringy-haired girls
smoke Marlboros, pacing
like restless alley cats,
biding time till something happens
to lure them away from
their concrete islands of ennui.

Sun, the Savior

He wakes up hung over
in a dark motel room
in Wherethefuckami, Ohio.
Tired, stiff, feeling
a hundred years old, he plods to
the bathroom to check the mirror
to see if all parts are intact.

His road roommate laughs,
enjoying this stumble
out of alcoholic haze.
Yellow light emerges through the curtains,
making the room cheery. If it wasn't
for the sun, this place would be
dreary enough to commit suicide in.

The Silent Witness of Mauthausen

Full
massive stones
inspired a private business
the Wiener Graben Quarry
on the lush Austrian hills above
the town of Mauthausen.

The intelligentsia crack and carry granite
O-n-e-H-u-n-d-r-e-d-E-i-g-h-t-y-S-i-x-S-t-e-e-p-R-o-c-k-S-t-e-p-s
   of the quarry:
Todesstiege (Stairs of Death).

Waning Gibbous
in front of fat twin guard towers
embedded into the high stone walls
the camp entrance gate opened daily
and forever swallowed the unsuspecting
KZ Mauthausen

yet outside the perimeter a concrete enclave
with a rusted ladder led to the drained bottom
of a swimming pool.

Third Quarter
or were they thrown in and shot
to death? Perhaps just a place of
leisure for the SS to hang out,
splash around and do laps.

Waning Crescent
at the gallows—its rusted wire still on
a pulley running from the thick
overhead beam down to an iron
handle—at the ready to plunk a human
and still after seventy-five years
paint-peels on the walls haven't fallen.

New
white tiled walls and floor—the morgue
with drain plates in the middle of the room
thick refrigeration coils covered
the height and length of one wall
cold storage for bodies to be dissected.

Waxing Crescent
on the dissecting room with the concrete slab
at a thirty-five-degree tilt
its small sidekick tub ready to hold
rotting emaciated organs

First Quarter
over the Ash Dump now
overflowing with wildflowers
the ovens of the crematoriums
have everlasting candles
burning in their mouths—
an aftertaste.

Waxing Gibbous
while they swam in the pool, smoked cigarettes,
and fucked prostitutes,
starving, thirsty, sick, diseased inmates listened
to the sounds of pleasure wafting above the horror.

Full
in the dark where the moon hangs
the silhouette of 380-volt electric barbed wire
leaves a scar across its face
while over ninety-five thousand people
were exterminated
hundreds committed suicide

the unflinching,
unblinking wide eye of the moon
saw it all
and to this day has never said a word.

III. Quizzicals

Trans-Portation

I run naked on the smooth,
hard-packed sand of the gulf
yet, far out over the water,
I also hover by a cloud
above a catamaran.

Behind me the surf laps
quietly over my run.
Down below, the beach stretches forever.
Under my feet the grit of blackened sand
blends into the brown
while the little red windsock
on the mast top tickles
my stomach.

Volare

Volare—I did not know what it meant,
And yet I drove an '82 Volare
Nine Volare years between New York and Galveston.

The Reverse Pavlov Effect

He had been away so long,
spending the summer at the home
of a friend who had a dog.

So long that, when he held the baby,
he scratched the infant's belly hard
and roughly patted his head,
as he had done to the dog.

No one seemed to notice.
When he caught himself,
he subtly changed,
softly rocking and stroking the baby.

Uncarved Epitaphs

A cemetery . . .

for	for	for	for	for
the	the	the	the	the
dog	duck	farmer	woman	carpenter
who	who	who	who	who
starved	couldn't	told	is a	said
	quack	me to	cuckoo	nothing
		moo		

a l l   c o v e r e d   i n   s w e e t   c l o v e r

My Subconscious Dreams a Poem

Brown syrupy liquid all over
the cab of my 1951 Chevy pickup—
on the road caramel oozed around the truck.

A large turnout of deaf people attended JFK's funeral—
mostly theater people, drinking Harvey's Bristol Cream,
while some actors signed monologues.

Just before a performance scheduled
at his father's elementary school,
he had to take a leak on the school grounds.

Geraldo Rivera has flat feet shampoo.
The kitchen ran out of catsup, so we sat together.
People were throwing up with blood
shooting out of their mouths and nostrils, as if
someone inside their throats was squirting
a steady stream with a seltzer bottle.

Last night I taught Moe Howard of *The Three Stooges*
how to bowl with snowballs, and I hurt him by mistake.

The Seven-Hundred-Dollar Louis Vuitton Fountain Pen

testing | | | | | ||| |
feels like writing with a pin
I'd like to make the nib thicker
so that ink flows out easily

testing ||| | | | |
it's getting a little better
but still looks thin & watery
keep blabbing
till a steady flow of black
oozes out effortlessly

now I'm pressing lightly
to see what happens…
\ | / / / | | \\ ||

**if I press hard
the ink flows better**
/ / \ \ | ||

I promised my friends James and Leslie
I'd write something brilliant
with their gift.

Arson

A disheveled fat man walks through an alley lot carrying a sack overflowing with garbage. A Styrofoam cup falls out. Throwing the bag in a dumpster, he hitches his pants up and looks at the old Victorian house across the lot. Yesterday a fire ate away the roof and the second-floor rooms. A three-alarmer. In 92-degree weather, townspeople from all over came to witness the flames licking out of windows, firefighters carrying smoldering bodies while wooden beams crashed down all around. Took all afternoon to reduce the blaze to smoke. The man rubs his belly and walks away.

The Missing Tipping Point

It was like scraping green scum
off aquarium glass.
What would have happened
to the Cultural Revolution
if word had leaked out that it required two
Red Guards to shave Chairman Mao's legs?

Origin of a Pratfall

Banana thrown on the ground
once yellow and smiling
now rotting in a frown
waiting for the step
of some clown
to squish it
down.

Keep Politics Out of Sushi

California roll and Arizona roll
side by side on a plate—
blue state, red state
my palate can't tell fate.

Support Group

Don't let my glasses and my hair throw you off.
You see—I am undergoing chemotherapy.
All my hair has fallen out. This is a wig
I got from a Halloween store. My eyes
have bags under them—hence the
glasses. My outfit? You guessed it. My body
misshapen from the drugs. I'm not
here so you can pity me. I want to show how
people can have a sense of humor about their illnesses.
Sure—call me "Bride of Frankenstein!" "The Alieness
from Planet X!" "The Quadruple X Porn Star!" . . .
anything but the C word. Say it and I'll vomit
on stage right now. Anyone dare say it? Hmmm?

The Absentminded Tooth Fairy

His son's
baby tooth in
the medicine cabinet
near dental floss, mouthwash, toothpaste.
But why?

How to Make Fire

—For Kelvin

I.
In the desert outside Flagstaff,
he showed me dinosaur tracks in hardened mud.
The smell of burning mesquite led us
to a Navajo outdoor market
a couple miles off the main highway.
He bought me a plate of barbecued mutton
with Navajo bread and Diet Coke—
a recovering alcoholic,
it's all he drinks

II.
We once traveled to Romania.
Walking around Oradea, he in
Navajo regalia and porky roach headdress
used for powwows,
braided sweetgrass burning in his hand.
Smudging, he called it.
He gave money to beggars.
People stared as if an extraterrestrial
had alighted in the town square

III.
He made teakettles out of clay,
inspired by handling sheep guts
on the rez as a boy,
fires them up in a hole in the ground,
glazing kettles with Diet Coke, Sprite, sometimes piss.

IV.
At night, we hung out at his house
watching smoky Westerns—cowboys shooting Indians
the Red Man scalping palefaces.
Why rehash this travesty?
He was captivated by the omniscience of film
reeling out the rustic landscapes of his ancestors

V.
One night at Indian Guides camp,
the old head counselor had
trouble making a fire from scratch,
rubbing a stick furiously in stone
to create a spark that never came.
He brought out his lighter fluid
and squirted it all over the
tepee of wood, and set it ablaze.

The Proof of the Pudding

He loved rice pudding,
especially the way his mother made it.
When he and his girlfriend got married,
his bride cooked him rice pudding.
"Nope, not like my mother's."

His wife flipped through
another cookbook and
tried a different recipe.
"Nope, not like my mother's."

She would take her husband
out to eat at a fancy restaurant.
For dessert, she ordered him rice pudding.
"Nope, not like my mother's."

One of her friends, a gourmet cook,
prepared an extraordinarily
irresistible rice pudding recipe
when they came over.
"Nope, not like my mother's."

One day, his wife went to the A&P
and bought ready-made rice pudding.
When he wasn't looking,
she spooned it out in a bowl
and sprinkled on a little cinnamon.
"Yep, just like my mother's."

A Life Hack

First thing his mother does
after getting a hotel room—
she peels off the bed's coverlet.
"Sex dust—housekeeping
only washes these once
or twice a month, if that."

IV. Irrevocables

The Perfect Woman

At least once a day
on the balcony of his small-town loft,
he leans against the railing,
watching
the cars go by.

His gaze shifts across the street
to a fancy country store
with an antique wedding dress,
yellowing
in the display window.

It is twilight and the dress
glows white under the track lights.

He feels he is
wasting
his life, waiting.

The Morning Paper

At the kitchen table eating
waffles and strawberries for breakfast,
he reads a news item about a woman
dead in her own backyard.

"Her body was found at 10:40 a.m. . ."
a time people at work are on coffee break.
"She wore white tennis shoes, black acid-washed jeans—
a white T-shirt with a green University of Maryland terrapin:
Uncle Terp wants you."

He can't swallow.
Pieces of berry float around in his mouth.
"The victim was 5 feet, 2 inches . . .
her clothes partially removed."
He minces the fruit into smaller bits
and tries to ingest it, but can't.

He leans back in his chair and
glances between his legs,
disgusted that there's an erection.
Across the table, his eleven-year-old
daughter munches on a piece of waffle
while watching a video on her phone.

She looks up at him with a "what?"
Shame, guilt, sorrow, deep love
suddenly rush through him.
Mouth still full, he shakes his head to say, "Nothing."
She shrugs her shoulders and goes back to her phone.

He spits the strawberry pulp into a napkin,
folds up the newspaper, and throws them away,
except for the memory of the woman
who will never again sit down to breakfast.

The Cryptology of Love

her sleeping puckered lips
invite me in to connect
to take away her baby-breath
instead I lean over to kiss
the hollow of her cheek
a pulse in her neck taps out
a lover's secret code about ...
she turns and stirs with her feet

... if only I could decipher.

Alone and Breathing

His breathing is cold, smelling of rot.
He grabs a small vial from his nightstand—
breath freshener, "Cinnamint."
The drop of oil singes
as it seeps over death in his breath.

His girlfriend keeps a vial in her Volvo.
Steering with one hand on the wheel,
she takes off the top with her teeth.
The other hand dips out a drop
and sticks the little plastic wand under her tongue.
When she drops him off at work,
he gets a Cinnamint kiss.

He buys Cinnamint now.
She's not with him anymore.
Not much he has of hers
can he hold onto so.
Yes, a hand-painted Easter egg,
a hand-colored blanket,
a hand-made greeting card,
but . . .

nothing can bring back her breath

that came hot and alive after lovemaking.
As they wound down, his stomach on her back,
his arms cupping her breasts
their heartbeats jammin' together.

"Am I heavy?" She's asleep.
He slowed his breathing to match hers,

not even a drop of Cinnamint under his tongue.

The Way He Sees Her

"You see me as I would like to see myself:
a good woman,
sexy as hell and smart
to boot (you do see me that way,
don't you? Or have I just made a
complete jackass of myself?)"
He just read her twelve-page letter in bed—
it had come by express mail that morning.

"the air conditioner . . . awful, artificial cooling
tricks the body into being comfortable.
My body isn't buying it."

He props himself up and grabs
a recent color photo off his nightstand.
She's wearing a straw hat—
a warm smile framed by dimples.
Her left hand rests delicately
over her left breast. She's looking
at something off to her right.

"I feel like I'm cooped up
inside the apartment all day . . .
like I'm caged and straining
against the bars."

He lays the letter on the bed
and pulls the photo closer to him.
The blurred-green shrubbery
in the background complements her red hair.

Long metallic earrings dangle
close to her shoulders.

"I'm restless but unable to move.
Life is passing me by."

Her serene expression
contradicts this.
He can't believe she's
that same sexy, smart woman.

The Eyes of Ingrid Isabella

He wonders how they will reconcile
their cyber lives with the real one
when she steps off the plane from Austria.

As he writes this with care,
putting an I before ngrid
and an I with sabella,
he will know for sure when he
looks into the eyes of Ingrid Isabella.

November Rust

On an early winter night in Boston,
he goes out to his sleeper porch
and looks up at the sky.

Lead-gray clouds race
over the moon, or is the moon
racing behind the clouds?

He thinks of the breakup
with his girlfriend.
Again, he was the initiator.
It's becoming a pattern and
he wants to break it.

He leans against the screen:
the bristles of his beard poke
through into the night.

It hasn't been this warm since 1966,
when the temperature hit a record 75 degrees.

The wind blows through and he smells
a warm August breeze. When it stops,
the screen smells of November rust.

Missing Children

by Debbie Rennie

—Translated from American Sign Language by Willy Conley

STREET CORNER

A gesture: "Have a flyer, please."
Anonymous takes it.
"Have you seen me?"
such a cute, bright-eyed girl.
Anonymous shakes his head.

The flyer floats down
to the ground,
face up,
paper dead.

NICARAGUA

On a coffee plantation,
laborers work the land.

A sweet young boy—
dark hair, skin, and eyes—
sows a row of coffee cherries,
one delicate bean at a time
as his father hoes and nudges him along

Out of the rainforest perimeter,
guerrillas advance with AK-47s,

chests crisscrossed with bullets
Zapata style.

Random rat-a-tat-tats send bodies flying
as the boy thumbs beans into the soil.
His father's body falls behind him.
A rebel grabs the boy's head,
twists him around, and shoves
a rifle at him—"Here!"

The boy offers a coffee cherry.
"HERE! Take the rifle!"
The boy holds out another bean.
"COCK IT AND SHOOT, BAM—HERE!"
Yet another quivering coffee cherry in hand—
"GO AHEAD! RAT-A-TAT-TAT HA-HA-HA!"
In slow motion, the boy makes one last
coffee bean peace offering
as the guerrilla triggers the automatic.

SOUTH AFRICA

A tribal procession:
in rhythmic, rock-a-bye cadence
pallbearers cradle a small coffin overhead—
an infant inside,
thumb still in the mouth,
the sleep of eternity.
Throngs of mourners follow.

Someone looks back and screams.
They turn the coffin in the other direction.
The crowd disperses.

A police van drives up,
lights revolving.
A door slides open.
A rifle fires at the congregation
riddling the backs of pallbearers.
A slug splinters the coffin.

IRELAND

A cute little lad with curly red hair—
freckled face with blue eyes—
walks eagerly beside his father.

Father takes out a bottle and takes a swig.
Son takes out a bottle and takes a swig.
Father fills his bottle with gunpowder.
Son fills his bottle with gunpowder.
Father corks his bottle with a fuse.
Son corks his bottle with a fuse.
Father lights the fuse.
Son lights the fuse.
Father throws his bottle.
Son throws his bottle.

Across the way,
a little blond in pigtails and bows
sits on the ground, playing Jacks.
She looks up at her father nearby
holstering a gun and taking a drag on a cigarette
before stubbing it out.

The girl giggles at her daddy
and goes back to her game.

As she tosses the little ball up
and snatches the metal star pieces,
the father-and-son Molotov cocktails
land in front of her.

STREET CORNER

Another Anonymous picks up
discarded flyers on the ground
shuffles through pictures of
"Have You Seen Me?"
      —smiling blonde-haired girl in pigtails
      —brown boy with coffee bean
      —thumb-sucking infant
      —boy with curly red hair
      —smiling blonde girl in pigtails

Anonymous shakes her head.

Flyers float down
to the ground,
face up,
paper dead.

Yew in the Family Plot

the roots
'neath family
connecting bone to bone
reach out, taking care of them all
for you

Uncle George

under a full moon soft crabbing
net in one hand poised for nabbing
flashlight in the other
wading a beam through brackish waters
in search of sloughing peelers
and elusive solutions to family sorrows

V. Environmentals

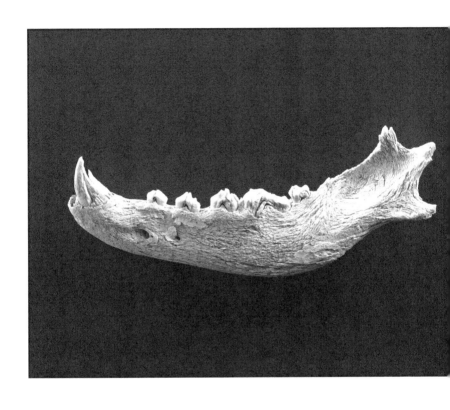

Five Haiku

coyote bones
scattered along the arroyo
rainstorm to the north

✦ ✦ ✦ ✦

rock-gray clouds creep south
while the snow geese migrate north—
buds can't wait for sun

✦ ✦ ✦ ✦

water over rocks
smoothing day in and day out
nature's sandpaper

✦ ✦ ✦ ✦

hawk atop the goalpost
scanning for football field mice
through yards of fake turf

high above the bay
lightning rips the sky like paper
crumples up thunder

A Maryland Eastern Shore Life

Salted steamed crabs
spread out on the kitchen table
of my childhood.

Beyond the porch
I see the salt marshes
of my adulthood.

The Breezy Logic of a Nine-Year-Old

My son and I sat on a pier bench
on a windy twilight evening, digesting
after a crab feast, admiring the full moon,
its path of light shimmering on the water.

"Where does wind come from?" he asked.

Far away in the arctic mountains,
cold air from snow meets warm air.
When the two clash, it creates energy,
building turbulence over water, tundra, and arctic wastelands
where there are no trees or buildings.
The baby wind intensifies, blowing miles and miles
past our creek and on to the South.

"Maybe the wind was created from millions of people
burping and farting," he said.

Wouldn't the air smell rotten?

"No, it'll clean itself as it travels over land and water."

Family Happy Hour on Christmas Day

oysters
half-shell on ice
dollop of cocktail sauce
slurp the brine, savor the mollusk
alive!

Nature Photography

Through a grove of cedars
still as a statue
in swift, sparkling waters
a Great Blue moves [*into view*].

Step by step the heron forages,
its body swaying to and fro
with neck craning [*focusing*]
to spot a meal of minnow.

The yellow bill opens—
a sudden, downward snatch
on a striped bass and then— [*snap*].

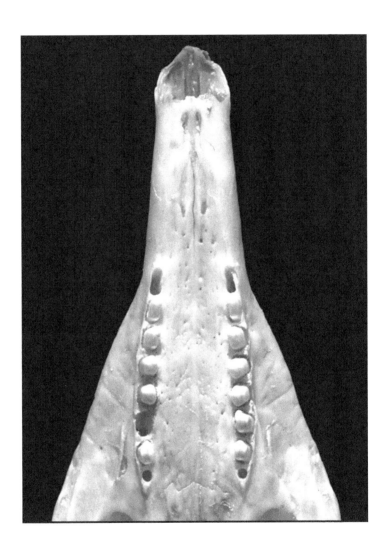

A Long Way from a Leper Colony

For beer and prize money
Texas pathologists raced
diseased, nine-banded armadillos
in a hospital parking lot.

Then these armored
critters were autopsied
in formaldehyde-fumed rooms
for research on how humans
contract leprosy.

Olfactophobia

She's sitting in seat 27F,
decked out in all-white sweats,
a vanilla shapelessness.
An air cushion, doughnutted around her neck,
blocks the view. The scent of menthol dominates the air.
Her hand rests on an Erma Bombeck book,
something about *The Sub-Total Woman*.
I shove my bag into the luggage compartment
and double-check my ticket.

I sit across the aisle and glance at her sideways.
Listening to a Walkman, her eyelids
grow heavy, her Tiger Balm
permeating my air space.
She pushes the recline button and leans back.

I see the clouds beyond the window thin out,
revealing a reptilian landscape,
my reason for flying to the Southwest.
My boarding pass says 27F, and I can see
that I will miss watching the desert terrain go by.

Juniper, Pine, Mesquite

Nothing—
the sun high,
the sky blue-wide.

Scraggly greens of juniper,
pine, and mesquite
encroach upon the rocky, red terrain.

The land guides me
down an arroyo
where my feet sink
into soft Southwest sand.

I sense something dart
from one sagebrush to another—
a flash flood,
a Mexican bandit,
a gun-toting landowner.

Nothing—
the sun high,
the sky blue-wide.

A few yards away in the dirt,
something white—a cow skull
with hollow, staring orbits.

As I pick up the skull,
I sense movement behind me—
a buffalo-stampede,

an Indian on the warpath,
a pack of coyotes.

Nothing—
the sun high
the sky blue-wide.

The Canyon

Someone once called it
the big hole in the ground.
So godlike and unreal
you have to blink,
stomp your feet,
inhale the cool air—
to know it's real.

Navajo Point, Desert View,
the colors, the patterns,
Hermits Rest, Cape Solitude,
the shapes and smells,
Point Sublime, Shiva Temple,
the depth and the breadth,
Point Imperial and Phantom Ranch,
the stillness.

Grand.

Vaudeville in the Insect World

A fat, black housefly
somersaults past
the open front door.

He rights himself,
dives for the kitchen window,
smashes into the screen.

Backtracking a few feet,
he whirls to the bathroom,
caroms off the light globe,
returns, eyeballs it, rotates,

careens into the living room,

whacks against the French doors,

shakes his head,

rebounds to the dining room table,

recovers on the morning newspaper:
"Managing the mortgage maze."
Shuddering his wings,
he breathes hard:
zzzzzzz zzzzzzz zzzzzzz.

The wind turns a page over him.

He thrashes around,
pokes his head out,
escapes to inspect
the rest of the house.

A dainty, yellow butterfly
flutters past
the open front door.

Subterranea

Underground where the 1, 2, or 3 goes by,
a homeless man is sprawled on a bench nearby.
People glance over to see if he's dead or alive.
Drool seeps out of his mouth
and drips between the slats of the bench.
It's 2:15 in the morning in New York City.

Constant chatter crackles from the overhead speakers.
A few out-of-towners snicker
at the garbled announcements.
The others stand around listless,
their minds leaving the station
until the 1, 2, or 3 comes.

A man at the platform's edge watches a rat
skitter from tie to tie,
dragging a piece of toast,
looking for an opening to
get to the other side of the tracks.
The man spits at the rat, but misses.

Further down the platform, a woman
wearing Cheese-Curl earrings
leans against a phone stall.
She nibbles on a soft pretzel with mustard on it.
The rat finds an opening under the first rail
and has two more to clear.

The man loses interest in the rat.
He picks his nose and looks at his find.

He puts his finger in his mouth and samples it.
The woman takes one last bite and
tosses the pretzel over the tracks to the other side
leaving a bit of mustard art on the tiled wall.
The tissue paper that came with the pretzel
floats lazily behind. The rat stops,
drops the toast.

A distant roar. It picks up the toast
and scurries to an opening at the next rail.
It turns the bread every which way
but the toast won't go through.
Ahead, light reflects off the rails.
The rat backs up and skips over a tie,
discovering another opening.
Same problem.

The light on the rails gets brighter.
Eventually the headlight of Number 1 scans
across waiting passengers before coming to a halt.

The man wipes his finger on his pants.
The woman licks mustard off of her fingers.
The train doors open.
People skitter out,
people scatter in.
The doors close.
The train vacuums ahead
through the dark tunnel.

The rat is gone.
Its toast flies up above the rails
and lands near the pretzel
across the tracks of the 1, 2, 3.

The Jay

"Naked as a jaybird"—
J-bird short for *jailbird*.
From bus to shower
prisoners forced to walk naked
one end of the prison to the other.

Jay—a country bumpkin
in the middle of the street
walking, gawking
at tall buildings:
jaywalking.

Back in the day, the Canada jay
warned Eskimos
of hostile Indians
approaching camp.
If Indians saw a jay,
they'd kill it.

Southern black folklore sees
blue jays as servants of the Devil,
flying in kindling every Friday
to keep his fire hot.

This morning, a blue jay
picked up a paper plane
from the middle of a juniper bush
and flew to its nest atop a tree.
Soon after, the paper plane dive-bombed
and crashed to the ground below.

Impressions

There.
Made visible, sometimes invisible,
some small as a sand dollar,
others large as a flounder.

A platoon—five little circles in line,
the fat one their leader,
all stand at attention outside a barrack
dented in the broadside from battle.

Puppies bark at it.
Lovers christen new sidewalks with it.
Kids track it across kitchen floors.
Artists imprint it for expression.
Dancers number its steps.
Lawyers argue its evidentiality.

If not preserved, nature will
abracadabra it away like the surf
washing a footprint down to
nothing.

Land of Lost Pets

Yet another sign tacked
on a pockmarked telephone pole:
"Lost Cat—If Found, Please Return."
Tigger isn't lost, she thought.
He's unhappy at home and ran away
to a place where pets hang out,
loll about, sharing stories
of why they're "lost."

Listening through the Bone

Five miles north of West Point
an American flag flies day and night
atop Storm King Mountain.
Its frayed fabric beckons him
on a hike from
Stony Lonesome Road
to see what it overlooks.

His map indicates it's the Hudson River,
flowing south. When wind
gusts up from the gorge,
the flag waves undaunted,

never lowered at sunsets or deaths
nor raised for sunrises or tributes.

The black of the Catskills
appears at dusk, while
lights from the Hudson Highlands
twinkle across the water.

He lies on the ground,
head against the flagstaff,
feet toward the river.

Listening through the bone,
he feels the flag hum and snap,
calling up Boy Scout days,
pledging allegiance to it—
standing at attention
during taps and reveille.

It's been pissed on,
trodden upon, burnt,
spray-painted, and worn.

Yet pine trees frame the clearing
where the flag stands, and continue to grow,
ever green. The sun soldiers on to rise and set.
The sky stays blue, the river runs on.

The flag fades, its threads unraveling,
but through his skull, he feels it flap
and flutter as hard as ever.